Living for Christ

ALBERT N. MARTIN
*Pastor of Trinity Baptist Church,
Montville, New Jersey*

THE BANNER OF TRUTH TRUST

THE BANNER OF TRUTH TRUST
3 Murrayfield Road, Edinburgh EH12 6EL
P.O. Box 621, Carlisle, Pennsylvania, 17013, U.S.A.

*

© The Banner of Truth Trust 1986
First published 1986
Reprinted 1993
Reprinted 1997
ISBN 0 85151 493 6

*

Set in Plantin, printed and bound in Great Britain by
Howie & Seath Ltd, Peffermill Industrial Estate
Edinburgh, EH16 5UY

Living The Christian Life

How am I to live as a Christian? That is a question of major importance. It is one thing to be certain on biblical grounds that I have life from Christ, but I must also be clear how I am to live the Christian life. My purpose in setting before you some of the major principles of living the Christian life is threefold:

1. I wish to sketch in a biblical theology of the Christian life. My purpose is unashamedly one of indoctrination—in the best and biblical sense.

2. I wish to inoculate you, and to immunize you against the major false views of the Christian life. Some of us desperately wish we had received such an inoculation early in our Christian experience. We spent many years chasing rabbits that we could never catch. We pursued experiences and states of mind and heart in the hope that somehow, in so doing, we would find what it really meant to live as a Christian. But we were disappointed.

3. I wish to purge you of any existing misconceptions which you may have about the Christian life. That may not be a pleasant experience, but it is in your own best interests.

1. NO ONE MASTER KEY

There is no one master key to living the Christian life. The kind of teaching I have in mind here goes something like this: Here is a Christian who for many years has found himself in the doldrums. He has had his sails hoisted, but he gets nowhere. He seems to know little of the wind of the Spirit carrying him along. Although his sails are hoisted, they seem for ever to be full of holes. While others around him appear to be making progress, he seems to remain motionless.

But one day at a conference, or while reading a book, or engaged in his own private devotions, he comes across a passage of Scripture which changes everything. For example he reads in John 15 that the Christian's relationship to Christ is like the relationship of a branch to a vine. This so ignites his spiritual life that, almost overnight, he is lifted to an entirely new plane of spiritual vitality. The holes in his sails have been mended! It is as though a mighty gale from God fills his sails, causing them to billow out to the full. In consequence he makes more substantial progress in the Christian life in six months than he has made in the previous six years.

He then tells others that the master key to the Christian life is the understanding of John 15. He is convinced that if only others will come to understand that Christ's relationship to his people is like that of the vine to the branch, they too will come to an entirely new plane of spiritual vitality and reality in their Christian walk.

Or again, think of someone who has been struggling with a besetting sin which leaves him continually bowed down and crippled with guilt. Unknown to others he is constantly bogged down. His wheels are up to their hub-caps in mud, and no matter how much he changes the gears and pushes down on the accelerator, he simply spins his wheels, and uses up his fuel and his nervous energy!

One day, however, at a conference, or reading a book, or engaged in his own devotions, he comes to Romans chapter 6. He reads that, in union with Christ, all that he was as 'old man' has been put to death, and the totality of the old life has been buried in Christ's tomb. He is now a new man in Jesus Christ. He sees that he is called upon to reckon it so, and to live now as one alive from the dead. He reads the words, 'Sin shall not exercise lordship over you'. He is no longer in the realm of law, under condemnation, and guilt, and all their crippling power; he is within the orbit and the dynamics of grace! What has happened? In faith's appropriation of the teaching of Romans 6, the wheels are suddenly out of the mud. The troubled driver is on solid tarmac, and when he gets into gear and presses on the accelerator he begins to move. Then, to everyone he meets he says, 'Do you know what the key to the Christian life is? It is to be found, as I myself found it, in Romans chapter 6.'

Do you know what a master key is? It is the key that will unlock any door. But there is no one master key for the living of the Christian life. The Bible nowhere presents us with one. Instead it provides us with a key ring on which is hung every text in the Bible. Our Lord said, 'Man shall not live by bread alone But by what? 'By *every* word that proceeds out of the mouth of God' (Matt. 4.4, quoting Deut. 8.3). If you are to be a whole Christian you need the whole of the Word of God, not one supposed master key.

Paul makes the same point: 'All scripture is breathed out of God, and is also profitable for teaching, for reproof, for correction, for child-training in righteousness, that the man of God may be complete, thoroughly furnished unto every good work' (2 Tim. 3.16-17). It is the whole of Scripture that is required to make men and women whole. *All* Scripture is 'breathed out of God, and *all* Scripture 'is profitable for reproof, correction, instruction in righteousness', in order that the man of God may be complete. We need the whole of the Bible to make us whole Christians.

Think of how the blessed man is described in the first Psalm. 'Blessed is the man'—negatively—'who does not walk in the counsel of the ungodly'. You want to be blessed? You will not be blessed if you spend hours in front of your 'telly'. For the most part the counsel of your television is the raw counsel of ungodliness, explicitly and implicitly. No-one makes any significant progress in grace who spends hours in indiscriminate television watching.

The 'counsel of the ungodly' comes through your popular tabloids—gossip sheets! You do not grow in grace, feeding your minds on that filth. 'Blessed is the man who does not walk in the counsel of the ungodly, nor stand in the way of sinners'. Do not tell me that you are growing in grace when you admire the utterly lawless patterns of life of big-name rock stars, and you let their drug-oriented, lawless, sex-soaked lyrics filter into your mind. You cannot and will not grow in grace if and when you 'walk in the counsel of the ungodly'.

That man is blessed who 'does not walk in the counsel of the ungodly, nor stand in the way of sinners, nor sit in the seat of scoffers.' Instead, his delight is in the . . . what? The one great key to living the Christian life? That is not what it says! The blessed man's delight is 'in the law of the Lord', that is to say, in the totality of God's revealed will. He meditates on the law of God day and night. 'He shall be like a tree planted by the rivers of water'. He shall be fruitful. He shall be one whose leaves never wither. He shall prosper in whatever he does.

There is no one master-key to living the Christian life. That view violates the entire structure of the Bible, particularly the Epistles of the New Testament.

What kind of problems did Christians in the New Testament have? Take, for example, the church in the city of Corinth. They had the problem of divisions; the problem of immorality; they had questions about marriage and about Christian liberty: shall I do this, do that, go here, go there? They had questions about self-denial and about spiritual gifts. If there were one master-key to the Christian life, would not Paul have handed out that key and said, 'Here it is. Whatever your problem is, here is the key'? But he said no such thing.

You need to be immunized against this teaching that there is one master-key to the Christian life. There is no one master-key, much as your flesh and my flesh would love to have one!

2. NO ESCAPE FROM TENSION

There is no escape from tension and conflict in living the Christian life. I am not saying that the Christian life is all tension and all conflict. The kind of teaching I am attempting to expose as fallacious is as follows: At a conference a speaker takes a text, out of context, *to which* he attaches or *from which* he extracts a shibboleth - perhaps he speaks about 'Christ living his life through us', or 'the saving life of Christ', or 'the abiding life'. Then the preacher, having expounded his theory of the Christian life, makes an appeal like this: 'Are you weary of the tension of wrestling with your remaining sin? Are you tired of struggling in prayer? Are you weary of having to battle with impure thoughts and thoughts of envy and pride and jealousy? Are you tired of this incessant conflict?'

What is the response? Every true Christian sits there, mouth almost agape, saying, 'O God, you know that I am tired, that I would give anything to have one day, just one day in which I did not have to do battle with dullness of heart, distraction of mind, and the seductions of sin that come to me from without and from within'. Then the speaker goes on to say, 'If you are tired of the tension, weary of the conflict; if you will but take certain steps, then Christ will so live his life through you that you will be freed from that tension and conflict. You will be so filled with the Spirit, so taken up in the Spirit, that tension and conflict will, to all intents and purposes, be a thing of the past as long as you maintain the posture of the abiding life. The moment you feel tension and conflict, it is because you have slipped out of that life and gone back to your old ways'. Now that is not a caricature. It is spelled out in page after page of book after book. Beware of such books! If you take them seriously, they could drive you either into a world of unreality or into a world of scepticism.

What proofs do I offer from the Word of God itself for my proposition?

(1) The reality of *indwelling sin* with its incessant and powerful actions upon us. Think of what Paul tells us: 'The flesh is lusting against the Spirit, and the Spirit against the flesh, and these two are contrary the one to the other, so that you may not do the things that you would' (Gal. 5.17). Paul does *not* go on to say that there is a way to be utterly, totally delivered from that consciousness of tension and conflict. He does tell us that we need not be *dominated* by the flesh: 'Walk in the Spirit and you shall not fulfil the lusts of the flesh'. But he nowhere says that the consciousness of the flesh's lusting will be negated; and where flesh is lusting against the Spirit, there is conflict.

I hold firmly to the time-proven interpretation of Romans 7.14-25 and know it to be the description of the agonizing daily conflict of a regenerate man. 'When I would do good'— and it is precisely at the point where I would do good—'I find another law in my members'. The more spiritual the activity in which you contemplate engaging, the more powerful will be the actings of remaining sin against it. You come home at the end of a busy day, and say, 'Well, I will just pick up *The Times* and take in a little news' ! Do you ever feel a powerful surge of indwelling sin when you propose to do this? I have never done so! But come home after a busy day, and say to yourself, 'I had only a few minutes in the Word this morning; I think I will sit down and read my Bible for half an hour'. What happens? All of a sudden lethargy comes over your mind and you say, 'I didn't realise I was so tired'. A dullness creeps over your mind and you feel so totally unspiritual that you think it would dishonour God to read his Word in that frame of mind. What is the cause of that? It is your indwelling sin.

When you take up the 'phone to talk to one of your friends you may be tired, but after talking for five minutes your mind is alert and your tongue is flowing at the rate of a mile a minute! But decide to go and spend five minutes in prayer, and what happens? Your mind is dull and distracted and your tongue feels as thick and lifeless as a piece of meat hanging in the butcher's shop!

God says that indwelling sin will be your unwelcome companion till the day you cross the river and enter the celestial city. That is the reason why there is no release from tension and conflict in the Christian life.

(2) Then, too, there is *the world* with is restless, aggressive pressure upon us. Paul tells us, 'Be not conformed to this world' (Rom. 12.2). J. B. Phillips' paraphrase accurately catches the mind of the Spirit in this passage: 'Do not let the world squeeze you into its mould'. This world's system is life in the totality of its organised existence, devoid of God. It is hostile to God's Word and law, in its standards, its goals, its opinions, its mindset, its people, and its philosophy. 'The world' is the totality of unregenerate humanity in opposition to God.

Scripture emphasizes that the world has never signed a treaty with those who have been delivered from it. It is aggressively and continually exerting pressure upon us to squeeze us into its godless mould. It is wild with rage when someone thinks and acts contrary to its accepted canons. It says that what counts is what you see, and what you have in your bank account, and what you have on your body, and what you have in homes and lands and material things. God says that what counts is the treasure that you have in heaven. He tells us that what counts is the hidden beauty of the heart, and of this the world knows nothing at all.

As long as the world exercises - as it always will - its aggressive restless pressure upon the believer there is bound to be tension and conflict. That is why the apostle John had to write, 'Love not the world, neither the things that are in the world. If any man love the world, the love of the Father is not in him. For all that is in the world—the lust of the flesh, the lust of the eyes, and the pride of life—is not of the Father, but is of the world. And the world passes away, and the lust thereof, but he that is doing the will of God abides for ever' (1 John. 2.15-17).

One of the things that is frightening to me (and I am old enough to have seen this happen) is this: I look out on the faces of young men and women, and I wonder how many of those who now show a refreshing, wholesome enthusiasm for the things of God will in ten years' time, be as dead as a dodo in spiritual things. What happens? Jesus said that some receive the Word as a plot of land receives good seed, but the weeds grow up and choke the plant. Do you know what Jesus said the weeds represent? 'The cares of this world, and the lusts of other things which enter in, choke the Word'. The world hates you if your life-style is in marked contrast to its own, and exposes the world's vanity. If you hold on to the things of this world loosely, and if you are not living for self and for station and ambition; if your great passion is that your life will be so controlled by Jesus Christ and poured out for the purposes of his kingdom that it will count and finally bring you to treasure in heaven, then you will be a constant irritant to the world, and the world will never be content until you are just like the ungodly. If you have got just enough religion to make you 'respectable', the world will love you all the more, because in that case you are a monument to its philosophy.

There is no escape from conflict and tension. But you may ask, 'As the years pass and habits of godliness are established, does not the problem become easier?' I can but say that, having lived half a century, and thirty-two of those years as a Christian, the battle rages more fiercely as I come down the other end of the road than ever it did at the beginning. John Bunyan had it right: there was no rest till believers were carried across the river.

(3) There is much to remind us that there is *the devil* with his vicious devouring intentions. Never forget Peter's exhortation: 'Be sober, be vigilant, your adversary the devil as a roaring lion walks about seeking . . .' to be a spectacle outside the zoo? No,

he is in business! The business of attracting attention to himself? He walks about 'seeking whom he may . . .' what? Simply bite and leave a few fang marks? Not at all! 'seeking whom he may *devour*'. He is out to devour you. That is why James says, 'Resist the devil and he will flee from you' (James 4.8). We find the same note in Paul's teaching: 'Our wrestling—our agony, our hand-to-hand combat, the agony of spiritual struggle—is not with flesh and blood, but against principalities and powers' (Eph. 6.12). Paul does not say that it is until you get a glorious baptism of the Holy Spirit, and then the warfare is all over! Or that it is until you go to a conference and learn the secret of the abiding life, and then it is all over! No! If you are a true Christian in touch with reality, the devil is out to devour you with an unprincipled, fiendish viciousness.

(4) We are saved in hope. We are saved in a context in which the best is yet to come. All we have now is the down-payment. Notice how this works. When God's work in you is finished, what will you be like? According to the Bible you will be like Jesus Christ. You will have a body fashioned like his glorious body (Phil. 3.21). You will have a spirit that is fashioned like his. You will not be God, but every last fibre of inbred sin will be purged from you so that you will have the ability to love perfectly in keeping with your capacity as a creature. Think of it! Going through not just a day, but a succession of aeons and never having a distracting thought, an impure thought, a jealous thought!

God has marked us out for that kind of perfection. We shall have a mind and spirit unstained with sin, a body capable of carrying out all the impulses of a perfectly holy heart. You know those times already when the Lord is especially precious and near, and you want to be free from the 'body of death' and serve him as angels do. The thought of an hour of unbroken communion with him is sheer delight. But you find as time goes on that weariness steals over your body and there is distraction and dullness. The fact is that we are marked for perfection in body and in spirit, but God has not ordained to give us that perfection here and now.

What is the result? Tension! Because we are saved in hope, and hope is not yet realized, there is tension, there is conflict. Imagine what it must have been like to be in a home where the apostle Paul lived or stayed on one of his journeys. If we could have sneaked up to the door of the room where he could be heard praying, would it not have been wonderful to hear the apostle at prayer? Yes, but do you know what it would have been like sometimes? You would have heard him groaning! You say to yourself, 'This cannot be Paul's room, I had better try another!' No, it is Paul's. He says, 'We that are in this tabernacle do groan, being burdened' (2 Cor. 5.4). There were times when he groaned because in that holy heart transformed by grace there was this burning passion to serve Christ. But he also had a body: 'The outward man is decaying day by day' (2 Cor. 4.17), and he groaned. Romans chapter 8 tells us the same thing: 'The whole creation groans and travails in pain until now; and not only so, but we ourselves also, who have the first-fruits of the Spirit, groan within ourselves, longing for the adoption, to wit, the redemption of the body' (Rom. 8.22-3). That sounds like conflict and tension! But rather than being a sign of an unspiritual frame, it is a sign of wholesome spirituality. There are groans and sighs that are the mark of a wholesome piety. There is no escape from tension. If you think that you have attained an escape from it, you are out of touch with reality.

3. NO SUSPENSION OF OUR FACULTIES

There is no negation or suspension of the conscious employment of any faculty of our redeemed humanity in living the Christian life. What are the faculties of a redeemed man? He has his hands, his feet, his eyes, his nose. He also has his intellectual faculties - his mind and his judgment, his emotional faculties of action, his volitional faculties, his will. He has his appetites, his feelings, his desires, and some of the psychological and physical ones overlap and inter-penetrate. These are the faculties of our humanity.

When God regenerates a sinner he creates no new faculties, nor does he kill or destroy any existing faculties. Grace works wonderfully and powerfully to give *new functions* and *new perspectives* to these faculties. God does not cancel, kill or negate any of the faculties, or create any new faculties. We are called to live the Christian life with the full engagement of our minds and judgment, the ability to think and to weigh and evaluate our affections, feelings, appetites and inclinations.

What teaching am I seeking to expose by articulating this principle? There are those who teach that, along with most Christians, your problem is that you are *trying* to live the Christian life, and God never intended that you should do so. Just as God never expected you to save yourself by going to the cross for yourself, he does not expect you to live the Christian life. All he expects you to do is 'to let go, and to let the Lord Jesus Christ live his life through you'.

I call this 'the funnel theory'! It tells you that you are to become totally passive, and then Christ will pour his life through you. He will live his life again in you and there will be the suspension of many of your faculties! The reason why you get so muddled is that you are using your own mind. You must not use it. Let your mind go into neutral. Let Christ's mind be your mind. The problem is that you are using your will and that it is getting in the way. Now negate your will and let Christ will through you.

This may sound very spiritual, but in fact it is a travesty of biblical teaching. I want to focus on three specific expressions of this kind of teaching:

(1) An imbalanced doctrine of the indwelling Christ

There is a doctrine of the indwelling Christ in Scripture: 'I have been crucified with Christ, nevertheless I live; yet not I, but Christ liveth in me; and the life which I now live in the flesh I live by the faith of the Son of God who loved me and gave himself for me' (Galatians 2.20). Many well-meaning people take these words along with such statements as 'Christ who is our life' (Col. 3.4); 'We are saved by his life . . .' (Rom. 5.10). Totally ignoring both the immediate context and the analogy of faith (the total witness of the Bible), they spin out a theory of the indwelling Christ. The kindest thing we can say is that this teaching is woefully imbalanced. It is a doctrine of the indwelling Christ in which, according to such authors as Watchman Nee, A. B. Simpson, and Mrs. Hannah Whithall Smith, Christ literally lives his life through you, even to the extent that there is the negation and suspension of your thought, your judgment, your will, and your affections; to that extent, they say, Christ will live his life successfully through you.

(2) An unwarranted deduction from analogies of the Christian life

Some of this teaching is derived from unwarranted deductions from the likenesses or analogies of the Christian life. Is the Christian life in one way or another like the relationship between a branch and a vine? Yes, but have you noticed what is done with that analogy? It is wrenched loose from all other biblical teachings. A whole theology is spun out of it.

I have heard it put this way: 'How many of you have ever walked by an orchard at the time when the fruit is coming to full bloom?' When people raised their hands, the speaker said, 'Now, let me ask you something. Did you ever see a tree agitated to bring forth apples? All the lovely little branches do is just hang there, joined to the main trunk, and the sap flows and the apples appear—and all the lush fruit of the Spirit will be born in a similar way'.

Others make their deductions from the biblical analogy of being united with Christ in his death, burial and resurrection, and they say, 'Are we dead with Christ? Well, if you go to a dead man and hold the most strongly smelling perfume under his nose, do you get any response? Of course not, he is dead. Or if there is a particular food that he was obsessed with in his life, you can hold it under his nose, but do you get any response? Of course not! So if you really are dead with Christ, sin will have no real and valid appeal to you'. These are unwarranted and unbiblical deductions from analogies of the Christian life!

(3) An inaccurate doctrine of sanctification by faith alone

The teaching goes something like this. When you were conscious of your guilt and stood under the condemnation of a holy God, and there was nowhere to flee for refuge, you were told that Jesus Christ, the incarnate Son of God, lived the life we should have lived, died the death we deserved to die, and on the basis of that life of perfect obedience culminating in his obedience to the death of the cross, there is a God-righteousness, a perfect righteousness, available to all who will believe. Then it may be said: 'What did you do to obtain that perfect righteousness? Nothing! you simply believed. The empty hand of faith took it'. 'Now,' they say, 'in just the same way, Jesus Christ is held forth for sanctification. What do you need to do? Simply believe. Faith operates in exactly the same way in our sanctification as it does in our justification.'

What is wrong with all those theories that have as their common denominator the suspension or the negation of the conscious engagement of all our faculties as redeemed men and women?

(i) They ignore the fact that in Scripture God addresses all our faculties with commands we are to fulfil

'Set your mind on things that are above' (Col. 3.2). Who is supposed to do that—you or God? Did the Lord Jesus say, 'If your right hand offend you . . . trust the indwelling Christ to make it rot away?' No! 'If your right hand offends you, cut it off and cast it from you' (Matt. 5.30). *You* are to do it! *You* are addressed. Paul said, 'I buffet my body, and I keep it under, lest in preaching to others I myself should be a castaway' (1 Cor. 9.27). Did he say that the indwelling Christ did it? No! '*I* buffet it . . .' 'Yield . . . your members as instruments of righteousness' (Rom. 6.13). *You* are to do it! I could quote dozens of texts in which every faculty of body and mind is addressed; for example, 'Flee fornication'. How do you flee from it? God says the best way to avoid fornication is by the use of your feet.

(ii) Mortification is said to be our responsibility by the Spirit

Paul says: 'If ye, through the Spirit, do mortify the deeds of the body, ye shall live' (Rom. 8.13).[1] All the biblical descriptions of the positive cultivation of Christian graces show us that it is *our* responsibility to cultivate them: for example, 'Besides this, showing on your part all diligence, add to your faith virtue, and to virtue knowledge, and to knowledge self-control . . .' (2 Pet. 1.5). You and I are to set our affections, our minds, on things above: 'He that says he abides in him ought to walk as he walked' (I Jn. 2.6). We are to walk in the Spirit (Gal. 5.16). We are to follow Christ's steps (1 Pet. 2.21). The positive cultivation of grace demands the engagement of all our faculties.

---

[1] I commend John Owen's dissertation on Mortification, in volume VI of his *Works*.

The dominant biblical images of the Christian life are military and athletic.

This is illustrated by many texts. But one text in particular epitomizes the teaching, Philippians 2.12, perhaps the most helpful text in all the Bible on this subject: 'So then, my beloved brethren, even as you have always obeyed [notice that he did not say, 'even as the indwelling Christ has always lived his life through you'], not as in my presence only, but now much more in my absence, work out your own salvation with fear and trembling, for it is God who is working in you to will and to work for his good pleasure'.

Notice the basic teaching. The imperative is this: 'Work out your own salvation'. Paul does not say, 'Work to attain it'. They were a forgiven people. They are to work out the implications; they are to work towards the completion of this salvation that is theirs in Christ. And they are to do it with fear and trembling, that is with the sense of God's eye upon them, and with the awful realization of the seriousness of the task. Why? 'For it is God who is working in you *both to will and to work* for his good pleasure' (v. 13). God's work in grace enables me both to will and to do, and it is because he is working in me to will and to do that I can work out my salvation with fear and trembling.

Well, does God work, or do I work? His working and my working are concurrent realities. His working comes to manifestation in my working, and my working is the proof of his working. Do you see the beauty of that? I need never fear that I will work out more than he is working in me. Our 'working out' can never outstrip God's 'working in'.

Another text in Philippians develops this theme: 'I can do all things through Christ who strengthens me' (4.13). Paul says, 'I can do'. How much can you do, Paul? 'All things'. In this context, 'all things' refers to all the things necessary in responding to the providence of God. The apostle says, 'At times I am in want, at times I am in plenty. Sometimes I have to learn what it is to be joyful when I amso hungry that my stomach is playing a tune on my backbone. At other times I am so full, I wonder if maybe I even verge on the border line of excessive indulgence, for I have been blessed with so much'. But, he said, 'whether learning how to be abased or how to abound in a godly manner, I can do all things'. 'I do them, but I do them through him who strengthens me from within'. 'I have been crucified with Christ; nevertheless I live, and the life which I now live in the flesh....' Who lived Paul's life in the flesh— Christ or Paul? Paul did so. But as he responds he tells us, 'I live it in faith in the Son of God who loved me and gave himself for me'.

4. NO CRISIS EXPERIENCE

There is no crisis experience promised or commanded as an essential element in living the Christian life.

Some teaching on the Christian life asserts that only a low level of Christian experience can be realized by the person who has not had a crisis experience subsequent to regeneration, or at least subsequent to conversion and to the beginning of conscious Christian experience. Furthermore, it is asserted that the crisis experience is both commanded and promised by God as the entrance into a qualitatively new dimension or level of spiritual experience, reality and power.

Throughout the history of the Christian church there have been many different strands of this crisis teaching. There is what we might call 'classic Wesleyan perfectionism', which concentrated particularly upon sanctification and spoke of a baptism of purifying fire, or of coming into a state of perfect love. It concentrated not so much on power for service or upon inward feelings, but on a crisis experience in which the power of indwelling sin was to all intents and purposes negated. I have read enough of classic Wesleyan theology to know that there are different opinions as to what John Wesley himself taught on the subject. But in a general descriptive manner this, I believe, is an accurate representation of old-style classic, Wesleyan perfectionism.

Then, too, there is 'the old Pentecostalism' in which the emphasis was upon a baptism in the Holy Spirit, generally subsequent to conversion, and invariably manifested by speaking in tongues: the way you knew that you had this baptism of power was that, when it came to you, you spoke in tongues. The primary focus in old classic Pentecostalism was the matter of power for service.

Thirdly, there is the modern 'charismatic movement'. Like classic Pentecostalism, its teachers use many of the same passages in the Book of Acts to support their theory of this necessary crisis. So they emphasize that in *most* cases—although there are different schools among modern charismatics—it will be manifested by the speaking in tongues. Some are content to believe you have 'got it' if you have a season of holy laughter. Others, however, say that you have not spoken in tongues because you have some psychological hold-ups, and if these can be removed the tongues are there. You just have not given them utterance. Here the emphasis is not so much on a baptism of purifying fire (as in the case of old classic Wesleyan perfectionism), or the baptism of power (as in the case of old classic Pentecostalism), but more upon a baptism of joyful praise-filled experience. I have been speaking of generalities, but I believe they are accurate.

Fourthly, there are the various forms of 'higher life' teaching. What they have in common is this: you are simply converted, simply united to Christ, simply regenerated, and then you come to a crisis of surrender and faith, in which 'you let go and let God' and appropriate the indwelling life of Christ. The common denominator is that it is a crisis without any external manifestation of tongues or holy laughter or shouting or jumping, but the end result will be new power to live a holy life—the emphasis falls upon the ability to be more efficient in the path of holiness.

Fifthly, there is a kind of teaching which has both old and modern proponents. It focuses on assurance, and has been expressed in terms of the biblical language of a 'sealing of the Holy Spirit'. Some of the Puritans—Thomas Goodwin, for example—taught this. There have been certain preachers in our own day who have believed this very strongly and emphasized it repeatedly. The basic concern in this teaching is that, subsequent to regeneration and conversion, there is a crisis experience in which the believer enters into a qualitatively new dimension of assurance by a sealing of the Spirit (some would say that the baptism in the Spirit and the sealing of the Spirit are synonymous). This results in a bright, new vibrancy in one's own spiritual testimony and experience; but the critical thing about such a person is that his true usefulness comes subsequent to his sealing in the Holy Spirit.

The above are five of the major strands of teaching, all of them with various sub-teachings also. But these are the main categories which teach that a crisis experience subsequent to conversion and regeneration is both promised, and some would say, commanded, as an essential element of living the Christian life.

What are the common denominators in all such teaching?

(1). Regeneration and conversion (some will often say *'mere* conversion') leave one inadequately furnished for living a biblically normal Christian life. The teaching runs something like this: 'Now you are a Christian you are saved, you are indwelt by the Spirit. Fine! But if you would *really live*, life with a capital L, live with power, live with overcoming grace, live with usefulness, live with grip in your testimony, you must have this higher, more noble, more glorious, more fulsome experience of

God's grace. Oh yes, you are converted, we agree, but this will not *really* make you different unless you have entered into this other experience. Conversion and regeneration will fit you to die, but they do not really equip you to live. If you are really to live, you need this crisis experience.

(2). An experience subsequent to regeneration is to be sought and obtained on the basis of meeting certain conditions or in the use of certain means.

Some who teach these various doctrines would say that the experience has to come to men unsought but, be that as it may, it is our duty to seek and to obtain such an experience, and in the pursuit of it to meet certain conditions. Each school of thought has its own set of conditions, and within each school there are differing conditions, but one of the common denominators is that the experience is to be sought until it is obtained after certain prescribed conditions have been met.

(3) All believers who have the later experience will know it because it registers at the level of Christian consciousness. A person may be brought to repentance and faith in a context of very poor teaching. Both adoption and justification are legal declarations of God, made at the very moment the weakest faith lays hold of the promised Saviour and the salvation that is in him. It is perfectly possible for a man or woman, boy or girl, to be as abundantly justified as the apostle Paul, and as much adopted as the famous Augustine, and yet to be unaware of it for lack of clear teaching. But all the proponents of the crisis experience theology say that this is not so as far as *this* crisis is concerned. All who have the experience will know it because it is registered in one's consciousness.

Now at this point the old Pentecostals were the least cruel because they said that a believer had an absolutely clear criterion by which to know that he had it—he spoke in tongues. Others who teach this doctrine and who do not give any criteria are cruel beyond words. They leave people saying: 'I must have this experience. If I am just an ordinary Christian without it, I cannot really become the Christian I ought to be until I have it. How shall I know when I have it?' But the basic answers of all schools say that you will know it because it registers in your consciousness.

(4). Behind this teaching is a very selective and questionable use of certain texts of Scripture. All crisis teachings claim to be based on Scripture and often the very language of Scripture is used to hold forth the experience. For example, one of the phrases which is almost a shibboleth in old Wesleyan perfectionism is 'heart purity', taken from Acts 15.9, 'purifying their hearts by faith'. In its context, however, it is talking, not about a second work of grace, but about the first work of grace that God performed in the hearts of Cornelius and his friends. Again, the concept of entire sanctification is taken from I Thessalonians: 'I pray God your whole body, soul and spirit be preserved entire' (5.23). The idea of 'the saving life of Christ', a well-known term in some teaching on the 'higher life', is taken from Romans 5.10: 'If when we were enemies we were reconciled to God by the death of his Son, much more being reconciled we shall be saved by his life'. A whole theology of a crisis of surrender in which we enter into the victorious life is couched in that biblical phrase and then strung into this terminology, 'the saving life of Christ'.

Thus one of the common denominators in all of these crisis theology theories of the Christian life is that the teaching is based on a very selective and questionable use of certain texts of Scripture.

How do we know that this teaching is not scriptural?

There is not one suggestion in the New Testament that any problem faced by any Christian or any church is ever resolved by urging them to seek a crisis of experience.

(1.) Consider the problem of divisions. There was a party

spirit at Corinth. Somebody did a little sanctified tattling to Paul—the household of Chloe. 'It has been signified unto me concerning you, my brethren, by them that are of the household of Chloe, that there are contentions among you !' (1 Cor. 1.11). Paul describes how those contentions were manifested. What can be more carnal than to find believers with a party spirit? These believers had all been 'baptized by the one Spirit into the one body', and had all been 'made to drink of the one Spirit' (I Cor. 12.13). They had a common experience in the Holy Spirit. There were not two levels of Christians—those who had only been converted and those who had been baptized in the Spirit; those who were only converted and those who had entered the higher life; those who were merely Christians and those who had had a baptism of fire. There is no hint in the letter of two levels of Christian experience. Paul writes to the church 'sanctified in Christ Jesus' and says, 'Now among you there are these divisions'. He describes the divisions. Some believers have attached themselves to Paul, some to Peter, and then the really spiritual ones said, 'We are the Christians, the real Christians, we are attached only to Christ.' But Paul puts them in the same class as the others.

How does Paul deal with the matter? Does he say that it is evident to him that the reason for the divisions is that they have never been baptized in the Spirit, that they have never come to grips with what it is to be cleansed from inbred sin? What does he offer as the antidote to this deep-seated and pervasive problem of division? He does not tell them to go ahead to get something more. Instead he urges them to come to grips with the truth of what they already are and what they already have. He says, 'Is Christ divided?' 'Were you baptized into the name of Paul?'. He shows them that they must come to grips with what they *already* have and *already* are. In the outworking of what they have and are the divisions will be swept away. You see the difference? He does not say, 'You must get something more'; he does say, 'You must understand and appropriate what is already yours in Christ'.

(2.) The problem of immorality. Paul's letter reveals that some of the Christians at Corinth were fornicating. They were living at a terribly low level of Christian experience, and they needed, if anyone did, a baptism of fire to cleanse them from inbred sin. Christians were even consorting with prostitutes, and possibly even with temple prostitutes. How does Paul deal with this terrible problem? He writes, 'Meats for the belly, the belly for meats, but God shall bring to naught both it and them. But the body is not for fornication but for the Lord, and the Lord for the body. And God both raised the Lord and will raise us through his power. For do you not know that your bodies are members of Christ? Shall I then take the members of Christ and make them members of a harlot? God forbid! Know ye not that he that is joined to a harlot is one body, for the two, said he, shall become one flesh, but he that is joined to the Lord is one spirit. Flee fornication. Every sin that a man does is without the body, but he that commits fornication sins against his own body. Do you not know that your body is the temple of the Holy Spirit who is in you, which you have from God, and you are not your own? You were bought with a price. Glorify God therefore, in your body (I Cor. 6.13-20).

Do you see what Paul is doing? As he faces this thorny problem of gross, moral deviation, he does not suggest that what these Corinthians needed was a qualitatively new experience of grace. He does not say, 'You need the baptism of the Spirit to purify this sordid, filthy propensity to fornication'. He suggests no such thing. Instead he says 'Do you not know . . . ?' (or in today's English, Don't you know . . .?). Think of what you are, think of the relationships that already obtained when in repentance and faith you were called into union with Christ. That was a real union: 'God is faithful by whom ye were called into the fellowship, the shared life of Jesus Christ. Do you not know that it is a real union? When you go to the house of the prostitute you go in union with Christ. Would you take the members of Christ and make them members of a harlot? Do you not know that your body is a purchased possession? When Christ bled and died, when he was inundated by the fiery fury of divine wrath upon the cross, he died to purchase you. Your hands, your feet, your sexual organs, are purchased property. O ye Corinthians, do you not realise it, do you not know it?'

Not once does the apostle suggest that the reason why the Corinthians lived in the way they did was that they had missed out on some crisis experience. He says to them, Here are the great indicatives—you are joined to Christ, you are indwelt by the Spirit, you have been bought with a price Now, what you need is not another experience, but to live out the implications of what you already are, and of what you already have. You can go through First Corinthians with all the problems of the church, and that is the emphasis that comes through again and again. You will find the same emphasis in all the letters of the New Testament.

I am not saying that believers do not experience spiritual crises; that would contradict both the teaching of the Bible and the evidence of Christian biography. Christians do have crises, and some of these crises bring them in a very short time to a level of spiritual reality and power that they have never known before. I am not debating that! It would be foolish to claim that Christians never have crises. What I am saying is that the Bible nowhere commands or promises a spiritual crisis of any kind as essential to living the Christian life. There is a world of difference between these two things. You can go right through the New Testament and notice how problems of every kind are taken up, at least in principle—moral problems, ethical problems, problems of inter-personal relationships, problems of indwelling sin, problems involving the world and the flesh— but never, never, *never,* do the apostolic writers command or promise a crisis experience as God's answer for these problems.

What then of the so-called 'four Pentecosts', mentioned in

Acts chapters 2, 8,10 and 19? We cannot expound these passages here, but I heartily recommend, for those who are serious in coming to grips with what they teach, reading F. D. Bruner's helpful book, *A Theology of the Holy Spirit* (Grand Rapids, 1970). There are one or two places in Bruner's book where a Barthian view of Scripture comes through. I do not hold such a view. He also takes what some have called a realistic view of baptism— some of us call it a sacramental view—grace actually meeting men in the water of baptism. But apart from those two flaws, Bruner's exposition of those passages in Acts is masterful. As far as I am concerned he gives an unassailable interpretation of the true significance of those 'four Pentecosts'.

I am not saying that a Christian should not pray that he may be more full of the Spirit tomorrow than he has been today. No! Am I saying that a Christian should not pray for a qualitatively deepened experience of the knowledge of Christ tomorrow, over and above that which he has today? No! As much as I abominate with all my being all of this crisis teaching which leads to confusion and, in many cases, to cynicism and fanaticism, I also abominate the spirit of Laodicea— 'rich, increased with goods, and needing nothing'—as much as to say, 'We have got everything in Christ; let us sit back . . .' . That spirit is nowhere taught in the New Testament. Although, in union with Christ, we have been 'blessed with every spiritual blessing in the heavenly places' (Ephesians 1.3), we shall spend our life-time working out and appropriating even the fringes of those blessings. At best we have only the down-payment; much is yet to come. God abominates the spirit of indifference: 'because thou art rich, increased with goods, and have need of nothing' our Lord Jesus said, 'I am about to vomit you out'.

We are to pray continually for more and copious supplies of the Spirit. 'If you who are evil know how to give good gifts to your children, how much more shall your heavenly Father give the Holy Spirit to those who ask him!' (Lk. 11.13). In Ephesians 1, Paul writes, 'Blessed be the God and Father of our Lord

Jesus Christ, who has blessed us . . .'. Then there is that theology in eulogy in which he blesses the Triune God for so great salvation, the Father for electing and predestinating grace, the Son for redeeming grace, the Spirit for sealing us to the day of redemption. Yet he proceeds in verse 15 to say, 'For this cause I bow my knees, that God would give you the spirit of wisdom and revelation in the knowledge of himself, that you may know what is the riches of the glory of his inheritance in the saints, that you may know what is the exceeding greatness of his power' . He says: 'You have all of this, but I plead with God that you may have a deeper, richer experimental knowledge of all that you have in Christ and all that Christ has in you'. As though that were not enough, in chapter 3 he says, 'I bow my knees' and then he prays for the unprayable. He says, 'I pray that God would make you strong to comprehend the incomprehensible, that you may know the length and breadth and height and depth, and know the love of Christ which passes knowledge, that you may be filled unto all the fulness of God.'

Paul is not praying that they will have some kind of a specific charismatic experience; he is not praying that they will have a second work of grace; he is not praying that they will have any of those five categories of experience that I have described, but he is praying that they will have enlarged capacities, expanded spiritual perception, and increased spiritual appropriation of the fulness that is in Christ.

The New Testament does not command us to seek, or promise us any crisis experience subsequent to regeneration and conversion. It does, however, teach with equal clarity that hungering, thirsting, panting, longing, pleading, yearning, seeking, advancing, are the characteristics of the healthy soul.

There are times when I despair and say, 'O Lord, is it possible that we can even expect to see people who have grasped that biblical emphasis?' It seems that people either go off on the one hand to all the excesses of crisis Christianity, or they drift off to this dull, lifeless, non-experimental, bland, cold kind of Christianity. Tragically, it often bears the name 'Reformed'. Frankly, I would rather be with a warm-hearted, woolly-headed 'Wesleyan' who thinks he needed and has had a second work of grace, but who is hungry for God, than the man who can sit for hours and prove that there is no such thing, and whose heart is as cold as a stone.

5. DIVINE CHASTISEMENT

There is no escape from Divine Chastisement as an integral factor in the Christian life.
The author of Hebrews underlines this point: 'You have forgotten the exhortation which reasons with you as sons, My son, despise not the chastening of the Lord, nor faint when you are reproved of him . . . for whom the Lord loves he chastens, and scourges every son whom he receives'. If God, in grace, has adopted you into his family, then he has adopted you into the family of his chastened ones. 'What son is there whom his father does not chasten? If you are without chastening, whereof all have been made partakers, then are ye bastards and not sons.' It is the father of the illegitimate son who is ashamed of his fatherhood. He does not openly own his son. That is the son who is left without chastisement. God has no illegitimate sons. His true sons he chastens because he is committed to make them partakers of his holiness! 'Our earthly fathers, indeed for a few days, chastened us as seemed good to them, but he for our profit that we might be partakers of his holiness' (Heb. 12.5-8).

Never forget that God's basic purpose in redemption is to make us holy, not happy. 'Whom he did foreknow he did predestinate to be conformed to the image of his Son' (Rom. 8.29). There will be plenty of happiness along the way, but this passage tells us that 'no chastening for the present is joyous'. I never once spanked one of my children and then allowed him to dance a jig around the kitchen. No chastening for the present seems joyous!

This idea, that if you only have a certain experience you can have a thirty-two-tooth grin twenty-seven hours out of every twenty-four hours, is the curse of the charismatics! But what help is a plastic smile when a chastened child of God comes to you in bitterness of soul? You become a Job's comforter. You say, 'O your problem is, you do not have the Holy Spirit. If you only spoke in tongues, you would just go to your room and babble for an hour, and you would feel better'. That is no caricature. I have heard that Job's-friends' counsel given to people. By contrast, here is the principle you should write on your heart: *Until you are made into the perfect likeness of Jesus Christ you are bound to feel the sting of God's rod* . 'No chastening for the present seems joyous', 'Whom the Lord loves he chastens'; 'as many as I love I rebuke and chasten' (Rev. 3.19). I tell you, when God is chastening it is not always in terms of physical affliction. We must never view God's chastening exclusively in terms of physical and financial calamities. They may be chastening; they may not be. To me the worst chastening is the withdrawal of the Lord's countenance; when you pray and do not sense and know realized communion with God. What more bitter chastening is there for a true Christian than to be unable to engage God in conscious, delightful communion and prayer? I know of no more bitter chastisement than that ! That is enough to set any true Christian searching his heart and saying, 'O God, where have I grieved you that you have turned your face? Hide not your face from me in my distress. Lift up the light of your countenance upon me'. The Psalms are full of such teaching.

Child of God, face the fact that there is no escape from divine chastisement as an integral factor in the Christian life.

6. MEANS OF GRACE

There are no effective substitutes for the appointed Means of Grace in progressing in the Christian life.

These means of grace fall into two categories: (1) personal and private (2) public and social.

(1) *Personal and private.* We know what the personal and private means of grace are. Jesus prayed, 'Father, sanctify them in thy truth: thy word is truth' (John 17.17); 'Wherewithal shall a young man cleanse his way? by taking heed thereto according to thy word'; 'Thy word have I laid up in my heart that I might not sin against thee' (Psalm 119.9, 11). Secret prayer! Prayer, that mysterious and awesome, and yet, at times, delightful privilege! Here is one important cause of weak spirituality: 'You have not because you ask not' (Jas. 4.2).

Why are some of you still crippled with certain besetting sins? You have not because you ask not. You do not bring those sins in prayer to the blood of Christ and to the cross of Christ, and to the withering power of the Spirit of Christ. If you became more earnest you would see those besetting sins losing their grip.

There are no effective substitutes for the appointed means of grace for making progress in the Christian life. Hold fast to the private means—prayer, meditation upon the Word of God, self-examination when necessary, perhaps seasons of fasting, saying 'No' to legitimate physical appetites in the midst of a crisis when you need to give yourself to the earnest seeking of God's face, the keeping of the blood-washed conscience. Make Paul's aim your own aim: 'Herein do I exercise myself, to have always a conscience void of offence toward God and men' (Acts 24. 16).

(2) *The corporate means of grace:* 'These all continued stedfastly in the apostles' teaching, in fellowship, in the breaking of bread, and in prayers' (Acts 2.42). Fellowship, praying, sharing life together! If there is one place in the world where you ought to be able to feel safe in letting people into your heart, it is among God's people.

Fellowship is not simply sitting in the same seats, under the same roof, on the same day. Fellowship is shared life. 'Who knoweth the things of a man save the spirit of man which is in him?' (1 Cor. 2.11). How can I carry your burdens if you do not get them out where I can see them, to put my shoulder under them? Scripture says, 'Share ye one another's burdens' (Gal. 6.2). 'Weep with those who weep' (Rom. 12.15). How can you fulfil that if you have got that silly, carnal notion of the stiff upper lip? Where does God's Word say, 'Show the stiff upper lip'? Nowhere! Many Christians are emotional wrecks because they are not in a community where, when it is fitting to weep, they can weep, and have their brethren weep with them! I suspect that some of my most effective pastoral counselling has come, not out of my mouth but out of my tear ducts when I have just sat with a weeping brother or sister, and wept and sobbed with them. It was all I could do. Their pain was too deep to be reached with words. That is fellowship!

May God help us to pray, and to labour to see churches formed where people will not run after the charismatics because at least it seems as though they have some 'felt' religion! I think I would run there, if my theology would let me, if I had to exist in some of the so-called 'Reformed Churches' that I have been in. The chill goes to one's bones like Highland weather. You would not dare weep, for you would be afraid the whole structure would be brought tumbling down by a tear shed within its walls. I do not mean to caricature what I have experienced, but it is true. The public means of grace which God has given is the church—a caring, loving, weeping, rejoicing, serving, evangelizing body of God's people.

These private and public means are God's appointed means. There are no effective substitutes for them as they minister to true growth in the Christian life.

Other booklets in this series:

The Authentic Gospel, *Jeffrey E. Wilson*
Behind a Frowning Providence, *John J. Murray*
Biblical Church Discipline, *Daniel Wray*
The Bleeding of the Evangelical Church, *David F. Wells*
The Carnal Christian, *E.C. Reisinger*
Christians Grieve Too, *D. Howard*
Coming to Faith in Christ, *John Benton*
The Cross – The Vindication of God, *D.M. Lloyd-Jones*
The Five Points of Calvinism, *W.J. Seaton*
Healthy Christian Growth, *Sinclair B. Ferguson*
Holiness, *Joel R. Beeke*
The Importance of the Local Church, *D. Wray*
The Incomparable Book, *W. McDowell*
The Invitation System, *Iain H. Murray*
Is There an Answer?, *Roger Ellsworth*
A Life of Principled Obedience, *A.N. Martin*
The Moral Basis Of Faith, *Tom Wells*
Open Your Mouth for the Dumb, *Peter Barnes*
Origins?, *R.B. Ranganathan*
The Practical Implications of Calvinism, *A.N. Martin*
Read Any Good Books?, *Sinclair B. Ferguson*
Reading the Bible, *Geoffrey Thomas*
Seeing Jesus, *Peter Barnes*
Victory: The Work of the Spirit, *P. Potgieter*
What is the Reformed Faith?, *J.R. de Witt*
What's Wrong With Preaching Today?, *A.N. Martin*
Whom Shall I Marry?, *Andrew Swanson*

For free illustrated catalogue please write to:
THE BANNER OF TRUTH TRUST
3 Murrayfield Road, Edinburgh EH12 6EL
P.O. Box 621, Carlisle, Pennsylvania 17013, U.S.A.